A TRUE BOOK™

Behind the Scenes
Race Cars

CODY CRANE

Children's Press®
An Imprint of Scholastic Inc.

Content Consultant
Matthew Lammi, PhD
Assistant Professor, College of Education
North Carolina State University
Raleigh, North Carolina

Library of Congress Cataloging-in-Publication Data
Names: Crane, Cody, author.
Title: Race cars / by Cody Crane.
Other titles: True book.
Description: New York, NY : Children's Press, an imprint of Scholastic Inc., 2018. | Series: A true
    book | Includes bibliographical references and index.
Identifiers: LCCN 2016048272 | ISBN 9780531235027 (library binding) | ISBN 9780531241455 (pbk.)
Subjects: LCSH: Automobiles, Racing—Juvenile literature. | Sports cars—Juvenile literature. |
    Racetracks (Automobile racing)—Juvenile literature.
Classification: LCC TL236 .C6975 2018 | DDC 629.228—dc23
LC record available at https://lccn.loc.gov/2016048272

All rights reserved. Published in 2018 by Children's Press, an imprint of Scholastic Inc.
Printed in China 62

SCHOLASTIC, CHILDREN'S PRESS, A TRUE BOOK™, and associated logos are trademarks and/or
registered trademarks of Scholastic Inc., 557 Broadway, New York, NY 10012.
1 2 3 4 5 6 7 8 9 10 R 27 26 25 24 23 22 21 20 19 18

**Front cover: A man waving a
flag at the end of a race**

**Back cover: A pit crew working
on a race car**

Find the Truth!

Everything you are about to read is true *except* for one of the sentences on this page.

Which one is **TRUE**?

T or F All race cars compete on oval tracks.

T or F Drag racers are the fastest type of race cars.

Find the answers in this book.

Contents

THE **BIG** TRUTH!

Under the Hood

**Racing at
Bonneville
Speedway**

Stock car
pit crew

Warning!
Some of these projects use pointy,
sticky, hot, or otherwise risky objects.
Keep a trusted adult around to
help you out and keep you safe.

**Laguna Seca
Grand Prix**

CHAPTER 1

Start Your Engines!

Race cars zooming around a track is a thrilling sight. No wonder people have been racing cars almost since the machines were invented. The first gas-powered automobile hit the streets in 1885. Two years later, the first car race was held in France. Early races aimed in part to prove that automobiles were a reliable way to travel. As cars gained popularity, so did auto racing. Today, millions of fans pack the stands at different races around the world.

German engineer Karl Benz created the first gasoline-powered car.

NASCAR's biggest race is the Daytona 500 held in Daytona Beach, Florida.

Stock Cars

A stock car has a much bigger engine than a regular car. Its parts are also specially designed to keep a driver safe while moving at high speeds. Stock-car racing is the most popular auto racing in the United States. The National Association for Stock Car Auto Racing (NASCAR) organizes the races. Most NASCAR races are held on oval tracks. During a race, stock cars can cover 200 to 600 miles (322 to 966 kilometers) at speeds of more than 200 miles per hour (322 kph).

Formula Race Cars

Formula 1, or F1, race cars look a lot like souped-up go-karts. Each has a single seat. Four wheels stick out from the car's body. The cars have a sleek design that makes them **aerodynamic**. This allows them to easily cut through the air. F1 cars can travel more than 220 miles per hour (354 kph). The cars race on specially built tracks or blocked-off city streets with many twists and turns.

The most famous F1 race is the Monaco Grand Prix. Cars race through the streets of Monaco, a country on the Mediterranean Sea east of France.

Drag Racers

In a drag race, two race cars compete side by side. They rocket down a short, straight track. The finish line is usually just ¼ mile (0.4 km) away. The fastest drag racers can cover this distance in less than four seconds! Their engines get a boost from a fuel called nitromethane. It provides as much as twice the power of regular gasoline. Drag racers can reach speeds of more than 300 miles per hour (483 kph), faster than any other race car!

A Racing Timeline

1887

France hosts the world's first car race.

1911

The first Indy 500 is held at the Indianapolis Motor Speedway.

Sports Car Racing

Sports cars are known for having two seats, two doors, and a lot of speed. Anyone can buy these vehicles for use in daily life. But many people also like to race them. The most famous sports car race is the Le Mans in France. Le Mans is an **endurance** race that lasts 24 hours. The focus is not just on speed. Cars must finish the race without any mechanical problems.

1929
Race cars speed through the streets of Monaco for the first Grand Prix.

1946
The first official Formula 1 race is held in France.

1949
NASCAR holds its first race at Daytona Beach, Florida.

Rallying

In rally racing, specially built cars speed headlong down unfamiliar, unpaved roads. Routes may go through forests, over rivers, and even along cliffs. Drivers cannot study the route ahead of time. Instead, co-drivers tell them details about the road ahead as they go. Turns, hills, and changes in the road surface are all important bits of information. They help the driver decide when and how much to turn, and when to speed up or brake.

Rally drivers often slide into turns on purpose. This is called a drift or oversteer. It helps a rally car turn faster.

INSIDE A RACE CAR'S ENGINE

An internal **combustion** engine powers traditional race cars. Gasoline and air mix inside the engine (see step 1 below). A round, flat piece called a piston pushes the mixture up (step 2). Then a spark from a small device called a spark plug sets the mixture on fire (step 3). That causes a small explosion. This happens hundreds of times per minute. The explosions force the pistons up and down. The motion turns rods, which turn a **shaft**. That shaft turns the car's wheels. VROOOM!

How a Combustion Engine Works

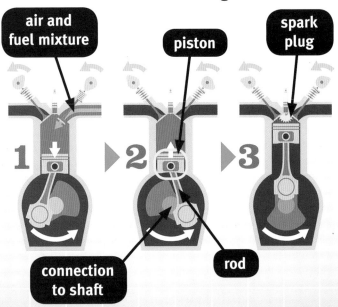

air and fuel mixture

piston

spark plug

1 ▸ 2 ▸ 3

connection to shaft

rod

smoke

CHAPTER 2

Need for Speed

Race cars need to be fast. But they also have to be safe. People called engineers help make sure both are possible. Engineers study the different **forces** that act on a race car. Then they find ways to use these forces to make cars speedier. That gives drivers an edge during races. Engineers also work to reduce certain forces to help drivers stay safer when traveling at high speeds.

 Car designers release smoke into wind tunnels to see moving air.

Drag is not all bad. Stock cars have flaps that open if the driver loses control. They catch the air to increase drag, slowing down a spinning or tumbling car.

flap

What a Drag!

The biggest force on a race car is drag. Drag occurs when air pushes or pulls on a moving object. A race car pushes through the air to travel forward. This creates drag. As the car moves, it leaves a "hole" of much thinner air behind it. Air rushes in to fill the space. This creates drag, too, as it pulls back on the car. Making race cars more aerodynamic reduces drag. A race car goes faster when air flows more easily around it.

Staying on the Track

Race cars are so aerodynamic that they need help staying on the ground. At high speeds, the cars can lift off like an airplane. To prevent that, engineers add pieces such as spoilers to stock cars and wings to formula racers. These parts create downforce. They slow down the air flowing over a car. Slower-moving air has a higher pressure. It pushes harder against the car's roof, keeping the vehicle on the track.

rear wing

Even with its rear wing, an F1 car might get a bit of air time.

The Art of Drafting

Drivers can take advantage of forces during a race by drafting. Drivers line up one behind the other just inches apart. The leading car pushes through the air in front. The next car fits itself into the hole of thin air left behind. As a result, the first car no longer has the pulling drag behind it. The second car doesn't experience the pushing drag in front. This allows both cars to go a few miles per hour faster.

The more cars there are drafting together, the faster they all will go.

Formula drivers feel forces on their bodies greater than those felt by astronauts rocketing into space.

Extreme Athletes

Drivers face tough conditions. On turns, they can feel forces five times that of Earth's gravity pushing on them. The sun, road, and a car's engine can heat the inside of the car to 120 degrees Fahrenheit (49 degrees Celsius). Drivers feel even hotter inside their fireproof suits that protect them in case of a crash. All these factors make it difficult to stay alert. Drivers need to be physically fit and have fast reflexes.

fuel can to fill gas tank

used tire being replaced

air compressor to add air to tires

Pit crew members work together to change tires and refuel cars in seconds.

Quick Stops

During races, a driver relies on a skilled team called a pit crew. These mechanics keep a race car running. They replace a car's tires and fill up its tank—all in a matter of seconds. They also make repairs to improve a car's performance. Racing teams in long endurance races have multiple drivers who take turns behind the wheel. It is the pit crew's job to make sure drivers make the switch safely.

SCIENCE

RACING FORCES

There is a range of forces that acts on all objects, including race cars. The forces include thrust (the driving power), **friction** (when two objects rub against each other), drag, and gravity. The opposite of gravity is called reaction force. It is the force of the ground pushing up on the car's tires.

Forces on a Car

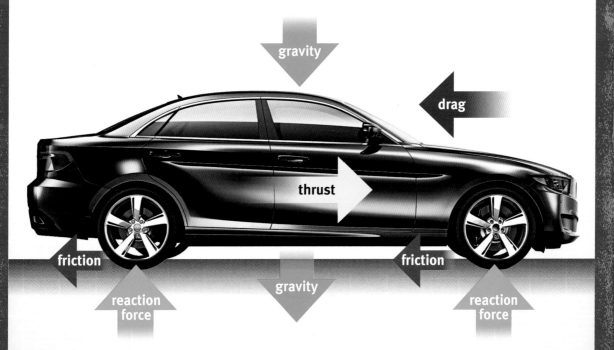

gravity

drag

thrust

friction

friction

reaction force

gravity

reaction force

F1 cars race around a winding curve during a Grand Prix race in Spain.

CHAPTER 3

Fast Tracks

Race cars compete on many types of courses. Some tracks are short, while others are miles long. There are courses with more than 70 twists and turns. Many tracks, though, follow an oval path, and race cars go around and around. Some tracks have hills, and some are flat. Some are made of concrete, and others are made of asphalt. Still other racetracks aren't really tracks at all. Different surfaces provide different levels of **traction**.

A grand prix is a major F1 race in a larger racing series.

Drivers have been setting records at Bonneville for more than 80 years.

Record Setter

The world's fastest racetrack is the Bonneville Speedway in Utah. The speedway is not a paved road. It is part of the Bonneville Salt Flats. This large, flat area lies in the desert. It is naturally covered in a thick, hardened layer of white salt. Each year, Bonneville hosts an event called Speed Week. Hundreds of people come to drive cars, motorcycles, and trucks as fast as possible. Many world speed records have been set here.

Long History

One of the oldest racetracks is the Indianapolis Motor Speedway in Indiana. It is one of seven superlong oval tracks in the United States called

The Indianapolis Motor Speedway was built in 1909, making it the oldest superspeedway.

superspeedways. Its 2.5-mile (4 km) track is home to the famous Indy 500 race. Formula race car drivers make 200 laps around the track during the event. They drive 500 miles (805 km) in total. That is about the distance from New York City to Washington, D.C., and back!

helmet

head restraint

The main threat to a driver during a crash is being thrown from the race car.

Road Safety

Extreme tracks call for extreme caution. Race cars have more safety features than regular cars. The most important is the roll cage, a metal frame around the driver's seat. It protects a driver from being crushed if the car flips over. Drivers also wear a safety harness. This extra-strong seat belt holds drivers tightly to their seats. A helmet protects a driver's head, and a head restraint wraps around the back of a driver's neck to protect it.

HARNESSING HORSEPOWER

The word *horsepower* is used to describe the strength of a car's engine. James Watt created this unit of measurement. He was an 18th-century engineer. Engines were a new invention at the time. Watt wanted a way to describe how much work they could do. He measured the amount of work a horse did in a minute and used it as a comparison. His idea of horsepower is still used today.

Under the Hood

A typical car **engine** produces 110 to 150 horsepower. A formula race car's engine makes about 900 horsepower.

A **cockpit** is where a formula driver sits. It does not have a roof and has only one seat. Heavy padding protects the driver.

engine

cockpit

wing

tire

chassis

A **chassis** is a car's frame. All other parts connect to it. Regular cars have chassis entirely of metal. Formula car chassis use a much lighter and stronger material called **carbon fiber**. This lighter weight chassis helps a car go faster.

How does a race car compare to the car that is likely parked in your garage? They both have all the same basic parts. But how these parts look and work are very different. Check out what makes a Formula 1 race car so special.

On wet days, formula racers use **tires** with **tread**. The tread channels the water so wheels do not slip. Racers use smooth tires on dry days. Smooth tires make more contact with the road for better grip.

Formula cars have two **wings**: one in front, one in back. As air moves over the wings, it pushes the car down onto the track. The wings also reduce drag.

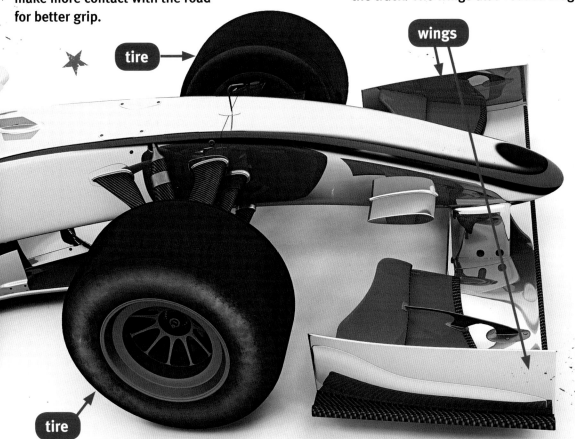

tire

wings

tire

Australia hosts the World Solar Challenge each year, inviting the teams from around the world to design and race the fastest solar cars.

The Future of Racing

Auto racing is the fastest land sport on Earth. But that has not stopped people from finding ways to make it even more interesting and exciting. Engineers are looking to make race cars more eco-friendly, or less damaging to the environment. They are testing out cars with unique shapes and technologies. And there are plenty of other innovations in the works, like robotic race cars.

Many World Solar Challenge teams are made up of students from universities.

Despite the dust and speed, there is no roar from this electric race car's engine.

Battery Power

Formula E held its first race in 2014. Typical race cars run on gasoline. Burning gasoline adds harmful chemicals to the air. But Formula E racers run on 150 brick-shaped rechargeable batteries, which don't cause air pollution. The batteries are similar to the ones that power laptops. Because they do not burn fuel, the cars are much quieter than regular formula racers. But they can still hit speeds of up to 140 miles per hour (225 kph).

No Drivers Needed

Cars without drivers might be the next big thing in formula racing. Roborace is a race for robotic competition cars that drive themselves. Teams create computer programs for their race cars. The programs tell cars how to steer through a course. Technology such as **GPS** helps the cars know where they are on the road. The same technology is used in **navigation** systems in regular cars.

Roborace cars don't need a cockpit for a driver.

The DeltaWing concept car (right) races around the track at the Laguna Seca Grand Prix in Monterey, California.

Test Drives

Engineers are always tinkering with race car designs. They often create concept cars that show off new ideas. They reveal these cars at racing events and auto shows. Auto shows are events that car lovers and car makers attend to see the latest vehicles. One concept car is called the DeltaWing. It has an arrow-like shape to make it more aerodynamic. It is just one of many designs race cars could have in the future. ★

NO NEED FOR GAS

Engines in Formula E cars are simpler than those in gas-powered racers. Electricity from the car's battery powers magnets inside the motor. The magnets cause a shaft to spin, turning the car's wheels. Because they have fewer moving parts than gas-powered engines, electric motors can accelerate faster. But batteries are heavy. Electric motors have to work harder to push the extra weight. That makes them about 1 second per mile slower than lighter gas-powered vehicles.

Hover Car

Friction is important for race cars. This force happens when two objects rub against each other. Friction helps a racer's tires grip the track to push the car forward. But too much friction can work against race cars, slowing them down. Try this activity to build a "hover car" using a disk and a balloon. It will glide over a surface on a cushion of air. Use it to see how friction affects moving objects.

What You Need

- ☐ pencil
- ☐ paper
- ☐ disk, such as a DVD or video game disk
- ☐ ruler
- ☐ cap with a pop-top from a water bottle or dish detergent bottle
- ☐ glue
- ☐ balloon

THINK AHEAD

Imagine that a disk is lying on a tabletop. You give it a gentle push. How far does it move? Now imagine pushing a disk that is floating just above the table. Which disk do you think will slide farther?

What to Do

1. Make a chart like the one shown below on a sheet of paper.

TRIAL	YOUR RESULTS
Disk by itself	
Disk with balloon	

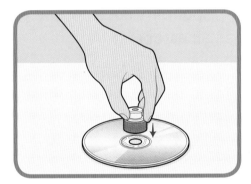 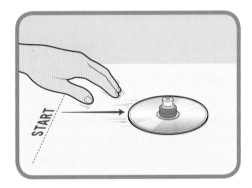

2. Make sure the pop-top cap is pushed closed. Glue the edge of the bottom of the cap over the hole in the center of the disk. Allow the glue to dry. It should form a tight seal.

3. Set the disk on a flat surface such as a tabletop. Give it a gentle push. Watch how it slides.

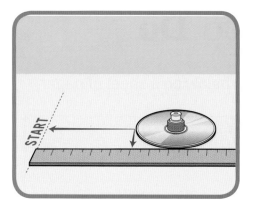

4. Measure the distance it travels with the ruler. Write down your results in your chart.

5. Blow up the balloon and pinch its neck shut. Fit the neck snugly over the cap's spout. Try not to let any air escape.

WHAT HAPPENED?

A. Which moved farther: the disk by itself or with the balloon attached? Why do you think that is?

B. How does the hover car reduce friction? How does this help it move?

C. Why might a race car that works like your hover car be a bad idea?

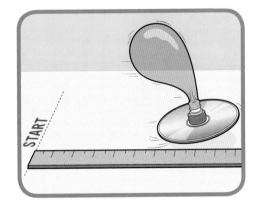

START

6. Set the disk on the tabletop. Gently pull open the cap's pop-top. The disk should hover slightly, creating your hover car.

7. Give the disk a gentle push like you did in step 3. Measure the distance it travels. Record the results in your chart.

THE TRUE ANSWER

When you push the disk by itself, it rubs against the table. The two surfaces grip each other. The friction slows the disk so it cannot travel far. Your hover car does not experience this friction. When you open the pop-top, air rushes out of the balloon and flows under the disk to lift it. Because of this, the disk does not rub against the table. It should glide farther than the disk by itself.

Clothespin Racer

Engineers are always looking for ways to make race cars faster. It could be a small change, such as swapping out tires. Or it could be a big change, such as giving the car a brand-new shape. Try this activity to build a clothespin racer. Then see if you can improve its design to make it speedier.

What You Need

- ◯ drinking straws
- ◯ scissors
- ◯ long twist ties
- ◯ four buttons
- ◯ clothespin
- ◯ glue
- ◯ tape
- ◯ long piece of cardboard
- ◯ piece of paper
- ◯ watch with a second hand
- ◯ 8 to 10 books

THINK AHEAD What features could help make a race car faster?

What to Do

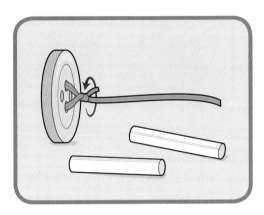

1. Cut two 1-inch (2.5-centimeter) pieces from the straw. Loop one end of a twist tie through two holes in a button. Twist the tie around itself.

 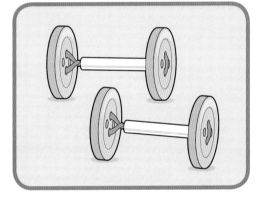

2. Thread the tie through a straw piece. Loop the tie end through another button and twist the tie around itself. This is one set of wheels.

3. Repeat steps 1–2 with the remaining straw piece, another twist tie, and two more buttons. This is your second set of wheels.

4. Glue the straw piece of one set of wheels inside the mouth of the clothespin. Let the glue dry. Tape the other set of wheels to the opposite end of the clothespin.

5. In an open area of floor, stack several large books. Tape one end of the cardboard piece to the top of the books. The other end of the cardboard should touch the floor. This is your racetrack. Place a piece of paper several feet from your track. This is your finish line.

WHAT HAPPENED?

A. Which car design was faster: your original one or your new one?

B. Think about your design changes. Explain why you think they affected your car's speed.

C. Auto races have rules about what features cars must have. That means some changes are not allowed. Do you think this is a good idea? Why or why not?

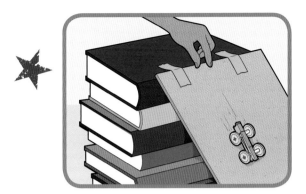

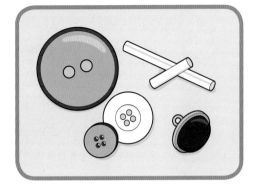

6. Test your car. Place it at the top of the track. Give it a gentle push. Time how long it takes to reach the finish line.

7. How could you make your car faster? Bigger wheels? A spoiler? Create a new car design and test it out.

THE
TRUE ANSWER

This activity requires you to think like an engineer. You start with a problem: How can I make a car go faster? Then you brainstorm solutions, such as using smaller wheels. Next, you test your design. Engineers follow a similar process to create better race cars. And they do not stop there. They keep going back to the drawing board. They make more changes and run more tests to improve their designs.

True Statistics

Amount of money that major Formula 1 teams such as Ferrari spend per season: $450 million–$500 million

Number of seats at the Indianapolis Motor Speedway: 257,000, more than any other sports venue in the world

Speed of the fastest car on Earth, the Thrust SSC, as of 2016: 763 mph (1,228 kph)

Estimated amount of fuel that cars use during the Daytona 500: About 5,400 gallons (20,441 L)

Average time of a Formula 1 pit stop: 3 seconds

Number of drivers to win all three top auto racing events (Monaco Grand Prix, Indy 500, and Le Mans) as of 2017: 1, Graham Hill

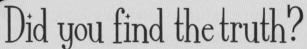

Did you find the truth?

F All race cars race on oval tracks.

T Drag racers are the fastest type of race cars.

Resources

Books

Aloian, Molly. *Racecars: Start Your Engines!* New York: Crabtree Publishing Company, 2007.

Mercer, Bobby. *The Racecar Book: Build and Race Mousetrap Cars, Dragsters, Tri-Can Haulers & More*. Chicago: Chicago Review Press, 2013.

Piehl, Janet. *Formula One Race Cars*. Minneapolis: Lerner Publications, 2011.

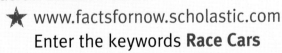

Visit this Scholastic Web site for more information on race cars:

www.factsfornow.scholastic.com

Enter the keywords **Race Cars**

Important Words

aerodynamic (air-oh-dye-NAM-ik) designed to move through the air very easily and quickly

carbon fiber (KAHR-buhn FYE-bur) very strong, lightweight material made up of fibers that have been treated with very high temperatures to turn them into carbon

combustion (kuhm-BUHS-chuhn) the process of burning

endurance (en-DOOR-uhns) the ability to do something difficult for a long time

forces (FORS-iz) actions that produce, stop, or change the shape or movement of an object

friction (FRIK-shuhn) the force that slows down objects when they rub against each other

GPS (GEE PEE ESS) short for global positioning system; a system of satellites and devices that people use to find out where they are or get directions to a place

navigation (nav-i-GAY-shuhn) the process through which people find where they are and where they need to go

shaft (SHAFT) the rotating rod that transmits power in a machine or engine

traction (TRAK-shuhn) the force that keeps a moving object from slipping on a surface

tread (TRED) the ridges on a car tire that help prevent slipping

Index

Page numbers in **bold** indicate illustrations.

About the Author

Cody Crane is an award-winning children's writer. She specializes in nonfiction and has written about everything from hibernating bears to roller coasters. Before becoming an author, she was set on becoming a scientist. Crane worked in different labs studying heart cells, making synthetic DNA, and testing blood for toxic substances. She later discovered that writing about science could be just as fun as the real thing. She lives in Houston, Texas, with her husband and son.